Tarantulas

by Eric Ethan

Gareth Stevens Publishing
A WORLD ALMANAC EDUCATION GROUP COMPANY

Please visit our web site at: www.garethstevens.com
For a free color catalog describing Gareth Stevens Publishing's
list of high-quality books and multimedia programs,
call 1-800-542-2595 (USA) or 1-800-387-3178 (Canada).
Gareth Stevens Publishing's fax: (414) 332-3567.

Library of Congress Cataloging-in-Publication Data

Ethan, Eric.
    Tarantulas / by Eric Ethan.
       p. cm. — (Dangerous spiders—an imagination library series)
    Summary: An introduction to the physical characteristics, behavior, and life cycle
of tarantulas.
    Includes bibliographical references and index.
    ISBN 0-8368-3769-X (lib. bdg.)
    1. Tarantulas—Juvenile literature. [1. Tarantulas. 2. Spiders.] I. Title.
QL458.42.T5E84   2003
595.4'4—dc21
                                         2003045559

First published in 2004 by
Gareth Stevens Publishing
A World Almanac Education Group Company
330 West Olive Street, Suite 100
Milwaukee, WI 53212 USA

Text: Eric Ethan
Cover design and page layout: Scott M. Krall
Text editor: Susan Ashley
Series editor: Dorothy L. Gibbs
Picture researcher: Todtri Book Publishers

Photo credits: Cover © James P. Rowan; pp. 5, 13, 17, 21 © James E. Gerholdt,
p. 7 © A. B. Sheldon; p. 9 © P. Goetgheluck-Pho.n.e/AUSCAPE;
pp. 11, 15 © E. S. Ross; p. 19 © James H. Robinson

Printed in the United States of America

1 2 3 4 5 6 7 8 9 07 06 05 04 03

Front cover: Small, gentle Mexican bloodleg tarantulas make excellent pets, but this rare spider is very expensive.

TABLE OF CONTENTS

Words that appear in the glossary are printed in **boldface**
type the first time they occur in the text.

TARANTULAS

The sight, or even the thought, of a tarantula is enough to strike fear in the hearts of many people. With its large body and thick, hairy legs, a tarantula looks like a dangerous spider! By creating giant tarantulas that attack entire cities, science fiction movies have made people even more afraid.

In reality, tarantulas are very shy. They do have a poisonous bite, but they are most likely to use it on small insects. Tarantulas usually bite people only if they feel threatened. Nevertheless, people are afraid of these spiders because they look so scary.

The normally gentle Mexican redknee tarantula looks so hairy and scary that it was used in *Raiders of the Lost Ark* and many other movies.

WHAT THEY LOOK LIKE

Tarantulas are hairy and huge. Some are bigger than your hand. Goliath tarantulas are the largest. They grow up to 10 inches (25 centimeters) across, including their legs.

Although, like most spiders, tarantulas have eight eyes, their eyesight is poor. Luckily, the hairs that cover their bodies help them "see." The hairs are so sensitive they can feel the smallest vibrations, whether on the ground or in the air. The vibrations tell the tarantula when something is nearby.

Like other spiders, tarantulas have eight legs. But unlike others, when a tarantula loses a leg, it grows back! Two claws and a pad with sticky hairs at the end of each leg make tarantulas good climbers.

This rose-haired tarantula's eight eyes are grouped together at the front of its body, but the spider's many hairs help it "see" much better.

HOW THEY GROW

Tarantulas are big spiders, and they produce big eggs. A tarantula egg is larger than a fully grown spider of almost any other **species**.

When a female tarantula is ready to lay eggs, she first prepares a small pad of silk. She lays her eggs, hundreds at a time, on this pad, then wraps them in more silk, forming an egg sac. The female guards her egg sacs until the eggs are ready to hatch.

Tarantula eggs hatch after six or seven weeks. The babies, which are called spiderlings, will leave their mother in just a few more weeks to start living on their own.

Tarantula spiderlings are tiny and white when they are born. They will turn darker in color as they grow.

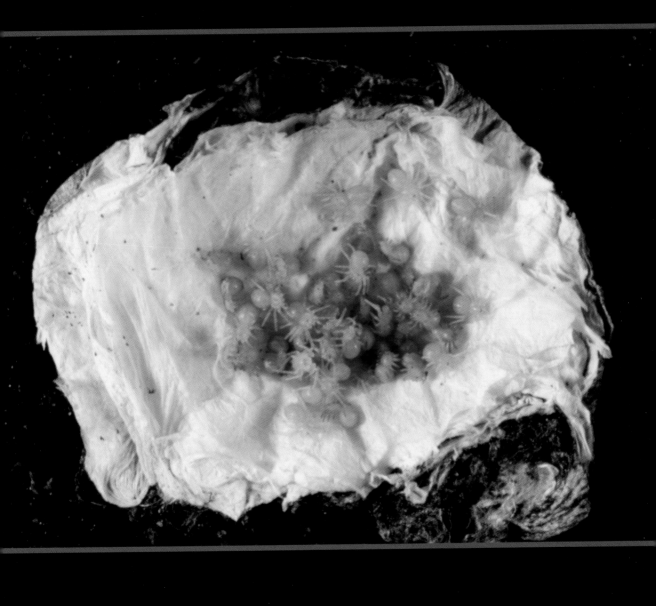

Like all spiders, a tarantula's body has a hard shell, called a **carapace**, to protect it. As a spiderling's body grows, it breaks the carapace. Then the spider crawls out, and a new, larger shell forms around it. This process is called **molting**. Tarantula spiderlings molt many times before they become adults — and it can take ten years to become fully grown.

As soon as a male tarantula is fully grown, it starts looking for a **mate**. But, because of poor eyesight, **mating** can be dangerous. A female will sometimes mistake a male for food!

Normally, tarantulas, male or female, live much longer than other kinds of spiders. Female tarantulas have been known to live twenty-five years.

This monstrous, multilegged creature is actually just a Mexican redknee tarantula crawling out of its outgrown carapace.

WHERE THEY LIVE

Tarantulas live in many parts of the world and on every continent, except **Antarctica**. Most, however, are found in areas with warm climates. Some live in dry deserts, others in wet jungles. The Goliath tarantula lives in the rain forests of South America. In North America, tarantulas live mainly in the southwestern United States and in Mexico.

The name "tarantula" comes from the town of Taranto, in Italy. Hundreds of years ago, people in this town were being bitten by a large, hairy spider. Scientists now believe that the guilty creature was actually a wolf spider, but the name tarantula lived on. Today, this name refers to a whole family of large spiders, but none are related to the wolf spider.

Zebra tarantulas are commonly found in the rain forests of Costa Rica, but they also live in the southern United States.

THEIR BURROWS

All spiders spin silk, but not all spiders build webs. Tarantulas live in underground burrows. They use their strong legs and **fangs** to dig the burrows. Then they line the burrows with silk.

Although they prefer warm climates, tarantulas do not like to be too hot or too cold. In the heat of summer, the burrow is a cool resting place. For winter, some tarantulas build a silk "lid" over the burrow's entrance to help keep themselves warm.

A tarantula spends most of its time inside its burrow. Although it rarely comes out during the day, it usually leaves the burrow at night to hunt for food.

Instead of a web, a tarantula lives in a hole in the ground that is lined with silk. This burrow was found in northern California.

HUNTING FOR FOOD

To catch its food, a tarantula relies on its senses and its speed, instead of a web. When its sensitive hairs warn that **prey** is nearby, the spider darts out of its burrow, grabs the prey with its legs, and bites down hard with its powerful fangs. The fangs **inject** deadly **venom**, or poison, into the victim's body.

Like most spiders, tarantulas eat insects, but they also eat larger prey, such as mice and lizards. Before eating any prey, however, a tarantula must turn it into soft mush. The spider's venom contains juices that **liquify** the victim's insides, but the tarantula also uses its strong jaws to crush the prey's body, which is another way to make it soft.

This very large tarantula is a Brazilian salmon pink birdeater, but what it really eats are crickets and other insects — and, now and then, a lizard!

THEIR BITES

Tarantulas bite with their fangs, but a tarantula's fangs are different from the fangs of other spiders. Most spiders have fangs that point toward each other and grab prey like a pair of tweezers. A tarantula's fangs are more like the fangs of a snake, which point straight down and stab their prey.

A tarantula's bite is poisonous enough to kill an insect, but it is not as dangerous to people. The bite of a North American tarantula is often compared to a bee sting. It might hurt a little and cause some swelling, but no one has ever died from it. Besides, tarantulas are shy creatures. They like to be left alone, so it is rare for a person to even come in contact with one.

As gentle as tarantulas can be, they still produce venom. For people who are sensitive to it, handling a tarantula can be dangerous!

THEIR ENEMIES

Big spiders like tarantulas make good meals for birds and snakes. These animals can catch and kill a tarantula before the spider can defend itself.

When a tarantula feels threatened, it will try to scare an enemy by standing on its back legs and showing its fangs. A tarantula also has **barbed** hairs on its **abdomen** that can be used as weapons. When the spider senses danger, it uses its back legs to brush these hairs at the enemy. The hairs fly through the air like small darts. When they strike something, the hairs dig in, causing pain.

Humans are a different kind of enemy for the tarantula. Although people do not hunt tarantulas for food, they do destroy the **habitats** where these spiders live.

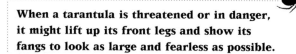

When a tarantula is threatened or in danger, it might lift up its front legs and show its fangs to look as large and fearless as possible.

MORE TO READ AND VIEW

Books (Nonfiction)   *Bird-Eating Spiders. Tarantula Spiders. Spiders* (series). James E.
Gerholdt (ABDO)
*Do Tarantulas Have Teeth? Questions and Answers about Poisonous
Creatures.* Melvin and Gilda Berger (Econo-Clad Books)
Interview with Harry the Tarantula. Leigh Ann Tyson (National
Geographic Society)
Spiders and Their Web Sites. Margery Facklam (Little Brown)
Spiders Are Not Insects. Rookie Read-About Science (series).
Allan Fowler (Children's Press)
Spider's Nest. Watch It Grow (series). Kate Scarborough (Time-Life)
Spiders' Secrets. Richard Platt (Dorling Kindersley)
Tarantula. Library of Spiders (series). Alice B. McGinty (Rosen)
Tarantulas. Early Bird Nature Books (series). Conrad J. Storad (Lerner)

Books (Fiction)   *Adiós Chi Chi: The Adventures of a Tarantula.* Nicole S. Amato
(Barron's Educational)
Tarantula Toes. Cul-de-Sac Kids (series). Beverly Lewis (Econo-Clad)
There's a Tarantula in My Homework. Susan Clymer (Econo-Clad)

Videos (Nonfiction)   *Bug City: Spiders & Scorpions.* (Schlessinger Media)
Nightmares of Nature: Spider Attack. (National Geographic)
See How They Grow: Desert Animals. (Sony Wonder)
Tarantulas & Their Venomous Relations. (Unapix)

WEB SITES

Web sites change frequently, so one or more of the following recommended sites may no longer be available. To find more information about tarantulas, you can also use a good search engine, such as **Yahooligans!** [www.yahooligans.com] or Google [www.google.com]. Here are some keywords to help you: *desert spiders, poisonous spiders, spider bites, spiders, tarantulas.*

www.desertusa.com/july96/du_taran.html

This page from the *DesertUSA* web site might be a little harder to read than others, but the information is well organized. Along with a description of the tarantula, topics include behavior, habitat, hunting, related species, and comparisons of species. The page also has some great photos, a QuickTime movie, and an interesting table of "Curious Facts."

www.enchantedlearning.com/paint/subjects/arachnids/spider/Tarantulaprintout.shtml

Visit this site to learn some basic information about tarantulas, including what they look like, where they live, and what they eat. This site also has a line drawing of a Mexican red-knee tarantula with labels and explanations of each of the spider's body parts. The drawing is printable, and you can even "paint" it with an easy-to-use, on-line color palette.

www.mpm.edu/collect/tar.html

Believe it or not, tarantulas are popular pets! If you are going to have a pet tarantula, however, you should know how to take care of it. This web site from the Milwaukee Public Museum in Milwaukee, Wisconsin, includes the *LORE* magazine article "Tarantula Care in Captivity" by Jody T. Barbeau and Martin J. Blasczyk. It will tell you how to house, feed, and handle a pet tarantula.

www2.tltc.ttu.edu/thomas/classPet/1999/Tarantula/facts.htm

This web page starts with a vivid, close-up photo of a Mexican redknee tarantula. The brief facts that accompany the photo are easy and fun to read. But the best feature on this page is a listing of the many different types of tarantulas in the world. African and Asian varieties, as well as North, South, and Central American species, are presented with both their scientific and common names.

GLOSSARY

You will find these words on the page or pages listed after each definition. Reading a word in a sentence can help you understand it even better.

abdomen (AB-doh-men) — the back half of a spider's body, which contains its spinnerets, eggs, heart, lungs, and other organs 20

Antarctica (ant-ARK-tih-kah) — the ice-covered continent that surrounds Earth's South Pole 12

barbed (BARBD) — having sharp, hooklike or arrowlike points that face backward 20

carapace (KARE-ah-pace) — the hard shell that covers and protects the soft body of an animal and the organs inside it 10

fangs (FANGZ) — long, pointed teeth 14, 16, 18, 20

habitats (HAB-ih-tats) — natural homes 20

inject (in-JEKT) — to force a liquid into body tissues through a sharp, pointed, needlelike instrument 16

liquify (LIH-kwi-fye) — to turn a solid into a liquid 16

mate (MAYT) — (n) the male or female in a pair of animals 10

mating (MAYT-ing) — joining a male and female animal of the same species for the purpose of producing young 10

molting (MOHL-ting) — shedding a covering, such as skin, on the outside of the body 10

prey (PRAY) — (n) an animal that is killed by another animal for food 16, 18

species (SPEE-sheez) — animal groups, each group having common characteristics and the ability to mate with each other 8

venom (VEN-um) — poison that an animal produces in its body and passes into a victim by biting or stinging 16, 18

INDEX